ATHLETIC ESPORTS

THE COMPETITIVE GAMING WORLD OF BASKETBALL, FOOTBALL, SOCCER, AND MORE!

by Daniel Mauleón

CAPSTONE PRESS
a capstone imprint

Edge Books are published by Capstone Press,
1710 Roe Crest Drive, North Mankato, Minnesota 56003
www.capstonepub.com

Library of Congress Cataloging-in-Publication Data
Names: Mauleón, Daniel, 1991– author.
Title: Athletic esports : the competitive gaming world of basketball, football,
    soccer, and more! / by Daniel Mauleón.
Description: North Mankato, Minnesota : Capstone Press, 2020. | Series: Edge
    books. Wide world of esports | Includes bibliographical references and index. |
    Audience: Age 8–14. | Audience: Grade 4 to 6.
Identifiers: LCCN 2019005957 (print) | LCCN 2019008210 (ebook) |
    ISBN 9781543573640 (eBook PDF) | ISBN 9781543573527 (library binding) |
    ISBN 9781543574517 (paperback)
Subjects: LCSH: Video games—Competitions—Juvenile literature. | Video
    gamers—Juvenile literature.
Classification: LCC GV1469.3 (ebook) | LCC GV1469.3 .M3763 2020 (print) |
    DDC 794.8—dc23
LC record available at https://lccn.loc.gov/2019005957

Summary: Describes professional video gaming and game tournaments including
Madden NFL, *FIFA Soccer*, *NBA 2K*, and more.

Editorial Credits
Aaron Sautter, editor; Kyle Grenz, designer; Tracy Cummins, media researcher;
    Laura Manthe, production specialist

Photo Credits
Alamy: PA Images/Adam Davy, 11 Top; AP Photo: Brian Mahoney, 6-7, Dan
Steinberg/Invision for NBA 2K, 22-23, 24-25, Frank Franklin II, 20, 27; Getty
Images: Chesnot, 28, Jamie Squire, 9, Miikka Skaffari/FilmMagic, 12, Ricky Carioti/
The Washington Post, 4-5, Tim Mosenfelder, 15; Newscom: REUTERS/Henry
Nicholls, 16-17, 19; Reuters Pictures: Elijah Nouvelage, 11 Bottom; Shutterstock:
EKKAPHAN CHIMPALEE, Design Element, glazok90, Design Element, LightField
Studios, Cover Top Right, Maryna Kulchytska, Design Element, Phojai Phanpanya,
Design Element, Roman Kosolapov, Cover Top Left, Rvector, Design Element

All internet sites listed in the back matter were accurate and available at the time
this book was published.

Printed in the United States of America.
PA70

Table of
Contents

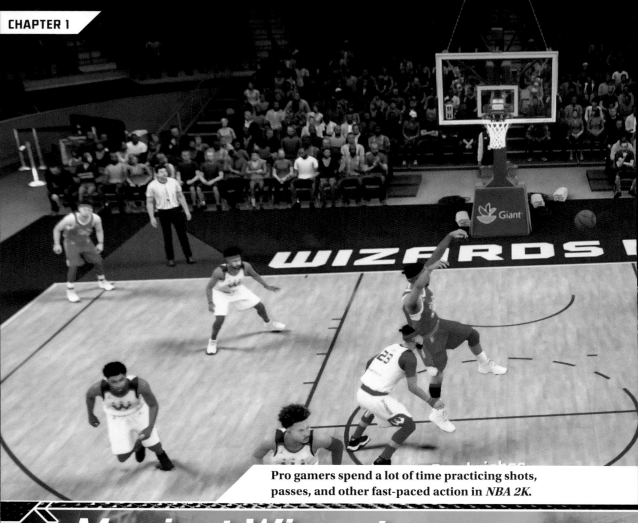

Pro gamers spend a lot of time practicing shots, passes, and other fast-paced action in *NBA 2K*.

Magical Wizards

It is game two of the Finals series and things are heating up. The Wizards won Game 1, but they'll need to keep winning to take home the trophy. Their opponents, the Pistons, have a 1-point lead. It's 66–65 and everything is on the line.

Only 56 seconds are left on the clock. The Pistons'
Joseph Marrero tries to pass the ball to a teammate.
But the Wizards' Ryan Conger cuts in quickly and
grabs the ball instead! He dribbles and passes it to
Maurice Delaney in the corner. Delaney shoots . . .
and it's good! That's three points for the Wizards as
they take a 68–66 lead!

A Whole New Ballgame

You might recognize the previous game and its classic basketball action. But you may not recognize the players. That's because this version of the NBA Finals doesn't take place on a court. It takes place in *NBA 2K*, an incredibly popular video game.

Welcome to the world of athletic esports, where classic sports action meets modern technology. Many people enjoy watching real-life sports such as football, hockey, and soccer. And many enjoy playing them as video games. Now fans can enjoy the best of both worlds by watching their favorite sport played in esports leagues and tournaments. Better yet, fans may even get to join in the fun and become competitive gamers themselves. Gamers must play and practice hard to become pros. It's a tough road, but the top players can make a good living competing in athletic esports leagues.

At big gaming competitions, esports fans can watch the action and their favorite gamers on several screens at the same time.

Fun Fact

Most players don't use their real names in competitions. Instead they go by gamertags or nicknames within the game.

CHAPTER 2

Athletic Esports History

Sports video games have been around since the 1970s. But their popularity really took off in the late 1980s. Early hits included games like *John Madden Football* and *Double Dribble*. Kids often played digital versions of their favorite sports on computers or game consoles. But the best players wanted a tougher challenge. They competed at local tournaments hosted by comic book and gaming stores. A few game companies even had official tournaments. However, such events were usually more about showing off a company's new game than testing the players' skills.

Fun Fact

There were once many sports video game titles. But over time the number of sports games has declined because of licensing. For example, without an official NFL license, football games can't use the names of real NFL players, teams, or stadiums.

licensing—the process of gaining permission to use the names, logos, and resources of another organization

In the mid-1990s, the yearly Madden Bowl quickly became one of the biggest sports video game tournaments. The National Football League (NFL) ran the tournament each year in the same city that hosted the Super Bowl. In the beginning only celebrities and NFL players were invited to battle it out and win a trophy. But over the years the competition saw great growth. Today *Madden* players compete year round to **qualify** for the Madden Bowl.

qualify—to earn a spot in a competition by scoring well or completing certain requirements

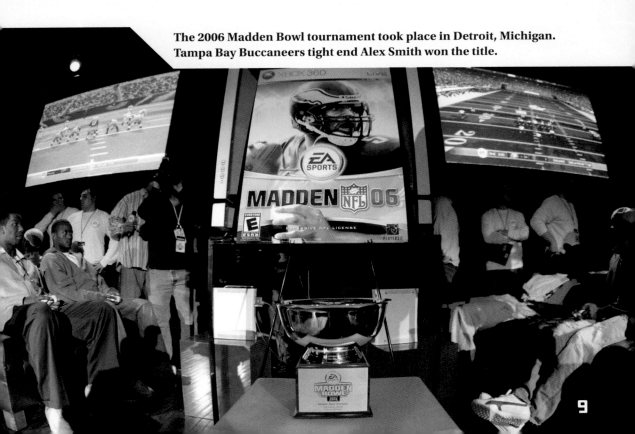

The 2006 Madden Bowl tournament took place in Detroit, Michigan. Tampa Bay Buccaneers tight end Alex Smith won the title.

Videogames Go Online

In the early 2000s, Sony and Microsoft released the Playstation 2 and Xbox gaming consoles. Suddenly, sports-based video game players could easily connect online and face competition from around the world. Game companies saw how popular the games were. Soon the companies started **sponsoring** more official tournaments to showcase their games.

In 1993 Electronic Arts released *FIFA International Soccer,* the first in the incredibly popular FIFA Soccer game series. The video game was based on the real-world International Federation of Association Football. The FIFA games became wildly popular. In fact, the game grew so big that in 2004 EA created the first FIFA Interactive World Cup (FIWC).

sponsor—to provide money or equipment for a player or team in exchange for advertising

Thousands of players around the world competed for a chance to play in the FIWC Grand Finals. In the end, Brazil's Thiago Carrico de Azevedo was crowned as the first FIWC champion.

Switch to Twitch

The video game streaming website Twitch.tv was launched in 2011. Since then the site has become the best place for video game fans to tune in to see their favorite games. The site broadcasts many large esports tournaments. By the middle of 2018, more than 15 million people were visiting Twitch.tv each day.

CHAPTER 3

Gamer "Serious Moe" won the 2016 Madden Challenge Championship in San Francisco, California.

The Madden Championship Series

The growth in esports created more interest in large gaming competitions. Since its creation in 2004, the Madden Challenge has continued to grow. In 2018–19 it was called the Madden 19 Championship Series and included four large events called Majors. Pro Madden players must spend several hours every day practicing to become the best and win the Major tournament prizes. Players in these events won more than $1.2 million.

Each Major is different in a few ways: how players qualify, which **game mode** is played, and the structure of the tournament.

Tournaments are organized as either group stages or **single-elimination** brackets. In group stages gamers play in small groups. Then the players with the best records in each group move on. In single-elimination play, gamers compete one on one. The winner moves on to the next round, and this continues until a single winner remains.

For Madden pro players, all roads lead to the final major—the Madden Bowl. The Madden Bowl prize pool isn't as large as some other Majors. But players are often seeking something even bigger—the glory of being named the best Madden player in the world.

game mode—a version of a video game that affects the game play in different ways

single-elimination—a type of competition in which teams or players are removed from play after a single defeat

Road to the Madden Bowl

Madden Classic

The first Major competition of the season is the Madden Classic. In this tournament competitors choose their favorite team and play in group and bracket stages. To qualify, players simply need to register online for the event until all 512 slots are filled.

Madden Club Championship

Players create a roster of their favorite athletes and compete online. The top players compete to represent their favorite NFL franchise. Only one fan representing each NFL team moves on to a live tournament in January. The Club Championship is the Major with the biggest prize pool overall: a whopping $700,000!

Madden Challenge

Madden Challenge is a mix of classic Madden and fantasy football. Players **draft** athletes to create a team and then compete against each other. As with the Club Championship, there are many rounds online before the best players compete live.

The Madden Bowl

There are many ways to get to the Madden Bowl. Players who won previous Majors all earn spots. Additionally, players can earn Madden Championship Series (MCS) points online or at the tournaments. Players who win enough MCS points also earn a spot in the Madden Bowl. In all, 16 players compete for the title in a single elimination tournament.

> **draft**—to choose a person to join a
> sports team or organization

Tournament	Number of Players	Roster	Prize Pool
Madden Classic	Group Stage: 512 Bracket Stage: 256	Competitors select any premade NFL team roster.	$165,000
Madden Club Championship	Thousands compete online; 32 players attend the finals	Players build their own team. They can choose any NFL athletes but have a "budget" based on NFL salaries.	$700,000 total; $100,000 for the winner
Madden Challenge	Online Group Stage: 256 Online Bracket Stage: 32 Live Group Stage: 16 Live Bracket Stage: 12	Competitors draft their players using an in-game trading card system.	$190,000 total; $35,000 for the winner
Madden Bowl	Bracket Stage: 16	Players build their own team. They can choose any NFL athletes but have a "budget" based on NFL salaries.	$200,000

Kansas City Chiefs defensive back Eric Berry won the 2016 Madden Bowl championship.

CHAPTER 4

Gooooal!

FIFA *Soccer* has been involved in the esports scene almost as long as *Madden NFL*. The soccer video game is the most played sports game in the world. FIFA is played one-on-one, with each player controlling an entire team. As the player switches between athletes, the game's **artificial intelligence** (AI) takes control of the other team members.

artificial intelligence—the ability of a computer or machine to think like a person

An International Sensation

When the FIFA Interactive World Cup began in 2004, thousands of players took part. But those numbers quickly grew. In 2013 the competition set a new record with more than 2.5 million players. But the amazing growth didn't stop there. In 2018 the FIWC became the FIFA eWorld Cup, or FeWC. That year more than 20 million gamers around the world tried their luck at winning the prize.

The FIFA eWorld Cup

To participate in the FIFA eWorld Cup a player must first qualify online. Playstation and Xbox players battle it out to earn Global Series Points. At the end of the qualifiers, the top 60 players from each console's **leaderboard** move on to the Global Series Playoffs.

During the playoffs the players earn their last Global Series Points. The top 16 players with the most points on each console's leaderboard then move on to the FIFA eWorld Cup.

The championship tournament is held in a different city each year. Players compete against others on the same type of console until one reaches the Grand Finals. In the final match the best Xbox player and the best PlayStation player play one game on each console. The player with the highest score wins the FIFA eWorld Cup championship.

Fun Fact

In 2017, *FIFA Soccer* was the best-selling game in the world.

leaderboard—a list of names and current scores of the leading players in a competition

Mosaad "MSDossary" Aldossary of Saudi Arabia claimed the 2018 FIFA eWorld Cup championship trophy and the $250,000 prize.

CHAPTER 5

Pick 1
ROUND 1
MAVS GAMING

RTREYO BOYD
Dimez
LEVELAND, OH

Artreyo "Dimez" Boyd was chosen as the first overall pick in the first NBA 2K League player draft on April 4, 2018.

Digital Dribble: The NBA 2K League

Like *Madden NFL* and *FIFA Soccer*, the NBA 2K League has a lot of esports fans. But there are some differences. Unlike games that feature a single pro gamer, playing in the NBA 2K League requires teamwork. Teams of players control separate characters in 5-on-5 games. It's important for teammates to communicate and work well together to succeed on the **virtual** court.

Fun Fact

In the 2018 season, 72,000 players qualified for the combine. The final league had only 102 players.

virtual—simulated on a computer or computer network

Making the Team

To join an *NBA 2K* team, gamers must first go through a four-part process.

Qualifiers

The first task players must achieve is to win 100 games online. They must also win at least half of the total games they've played. Winning 100 out of 500 games won't cut it.

Combine

The players who've qualified then participate in an online **combine**. Players select a position on a team and must play 25 games. Their overall statistics are tracked for these games. The best players then move on to be considered by a selection committee.

Selection Committee

The best combine players join with previous league players to form a group of the top 200 players. The selection committee then reviews the players' game stats. The committee also interviews players and checks their backgrounds to make sure they'll act professionally and be good role models. The committee then forms a 150-player draft pool.

Player Draft

Finally, teams take turns selecting from the draft pool. However, there are only six spots open on each team. Not every player will be chosen. After the draft, teams might trade players as well.

combine—an event at which scouts evaluate players who hope to be drafted by a professional team

Before there was an official league, teams could compete in the NBA 2K Road to the Finals for a chance at a large cash prize and a trip to the NBA Finals.

NBA 2K Season + Playoff Structure

Once teams are created, it's time to play! The NBA 2K League's first season in 2018 lasted for 17 weeks. Each team played 14 games during the regular season. The eight teams with the best records then moved on to compete in the playoffs.

In the first playoff round, teams played one game, with the winners advancing to the next round. In the semi-finals and finals, teams had to win 2 out of 3 games. In the 2018 Finals, Knicks Gaming topped Heat Check Gaming two games in a row to claim the championship.

Fun Fact

Throughout the season there were three additional tournaments. Winning or losing a tournament didn't affect a team's overall record. But the winning team could take home more money.

An Esports League of Their Own

Each *NBA 2K* team is owned and managed by a real NBA franchise. In the 2019 season there were 21 *NBA 2K* teams, each connected to a real-life team:

NBA 2K League Team	NBA Franchise
76ers GC	Philadelphia 76ers
Blazer5 Gaming	Portland Trail Blazers
Bucks Gaming	Milwaukee Bucks
Cavs Legion GC	Cleveland Cavaliers
Celtics Crossover Gaming	Boston Celtics
Grizz Gaming	Memphis Grizzlies
Hawks Talon GC	Atlanta Hawks
Heat Check Gaming	Miami Heat
Jazz Gaming	Utah Jazz
Kings Guard Gaming	Sacramento Kings
Knicks Gaming	New York Knicks
Lakers Gaming	Los Angeles Lakers
Magic Gaming	Orlando Magic
Mavs Gaming	Dallas Mavericks
Nets GC	Brooklyn Nets
Pacers Gaming	Indiana Pacers
Pistons GT	Detroit Pistons
Raptors Uprising GC	Toronto Raptors
T-Wolves Gaming	Minnesota Timberwolves
Warriors Gaming Squad	Golden State Warriors
Wizards District Gaming	Washington Wizards

All pro gamers in the NBA 2K League are paid between $32,000 and $35,000 per year. Players can earn more if they win in tournaments. In the 2018 season, the Knicks Gaming team earned an additional $300,000 for winning the championship.

CHAPTER 6

NBA 2K teams practice together many hours every day to improve their teamwork and prepare for every match.

The Pro Life

The careers of professional esports gamers depend on the games they play. Their training schedules and daily routines can be very different. But all pro players have at least one thing in common. They are very dedicated to becoming the best at their game.

Travelling!

NBA 2K pros live in team houses while playing. Each team house is located in the same city as the host team. Each weekend all the teams fly to New York City to play against each other at the NBA 2K League Studio. After a weekend of intense games, teams return to their houses to train for the following week. It can be a grueling schedule, but it's well worth it for gamers who want to win a championship.

For *NBA 2K* players, their weeks are filled with training and practice. They dedicate hours every day to playing online or practicing their in-game skills. Teams often play 3-on-3 games and practice premade plays against their own teammates. Sometimes teams will **scrimmage** against other *NBA 2K* teams. And just like real sports pros, teams spend time studying videos of past games. Game film helps them learn about their opponents and find ways to improve their own game.

scrimmage—to play a practice game against another team or other players

Are Esports Equal?

Esport competitions aren't tied to a person's athletic abilities. So it should be a space that welcomes all players, not just men. However, there are few women involved in the esports scene. One reason for this may be online or in-game bullying. Many female players have said that they've been insulted by fellow gamers just for being women. Because of this, some women choose not to compete in esports, no matter how skilled they may be.

The **commissioner** of the NBA, Adam Silver, was concerned about the NBA 2K League. In 2018 *NBA 2K* teams drafted 102 male players. Silver said he was disappointed no women were included. Silver and the 2K League reviewed the process for building the draft pool. They found that male players didn't pass the ball to female players very often. The league instead began focusing more on players' skills when they controlled the ball. The league also added rules requiring players to treat fellow gamers with more respect. As a result, several players were removed from the combine for making sexist comments.

commissioner—a person who is in charge of a professional sport

Fun Fact

In 2019 Chiquita Evans became the first woman to be drafted in the NBA 2K League. She was chosen with the 56th overall pick by Warriors Gaming.

Are You the Next Esports Pro?

If you're thinking about going pro, you'll need to do some research. Not all games have large tournaments or organized leagues. Look into your favorite games to see if there are any pro teams. Then find out how to compete. You may need to go through tryouts. Or you might just need to win a lot of games.

Either way, when you know what you want to play, then it's time to drill! Play the game regularly and work to climb the leaderboards. A pro team or player might take notice and give you some advice on how to get into the esports scene. Before you know it, you may just find your way to the top!

Young gamers who want to become pros need to practice a lot. With a high ranking, they may be noticed by a pro esports team.

Fun Fact

Recently some high schools have started creating esports leagues. Many play only action games, but one day they may include some athletic games as well.

Glossary

artificial intelligence (ar-ti-FISH-uhl in-TEL-uh-junss)—the ability of a computer or machine to think like a person

combine (KOM-bahyn)—an event at which scouts evaluate players who hope to be drafted by a professional team

commissioner (kuh-MI-shuh-nuhr)—a person who is in charge of a professional sport

draft (DRAFT)—to choose a person to join a sports team or organization

game mode (GAYM MOHD)—a version of a video game that affects the game play in different ways

leaderboard (LEE-dur-bohrd)—a list of names and current scores of the leading players in a competition

licensing (LAHY-suhn-sing)—the process of gaining permission to use the names, logos, and resources of another organization

qualify (KWAHL-uh-fye)—to earn a spot in a competition by scoring well or completing certain requirements

scrimmage (SKRIM-ij)—to play a practice game against another team or other players

single-elimination (SING-guhl ih-lim-uh-NEY-shuhn)—a type of competition in which teams or players are removed from play after a single defeat

sponsor (SPON-sur)—to provide money or equipment for a player or team in exchange for advertising

virtual (VUR-choo-uhl)—simulated on a computer or computer network

Read More

Hustad, Douglas. *Gaming and Professional Sports Teams*. E-Sports: Game On! Chicago: Norwood House Press, 2018.

Jankowski, Matthew. *The Modern Nerd's Guide to eSports*. Geek Out! New York: Gareth Stevens Publishing, 2018.

Marquardt, Meg. *Great E-Sports Debates*. The Great Sports Debates. Minneapolis: Abdo Pub., 2018.

Internet Sites

ESPN: Esports
http://www.espn.com/esports/

Madden Championship Series
https://www.easports.com/madden-nfl/compete/home

NBA 2K League
https://2kleague.nba.com

Index